13 Days With Gideon

The Story of Gideon William Briner

By: Harrison and Loni Briner

PRESS

Table of Contents

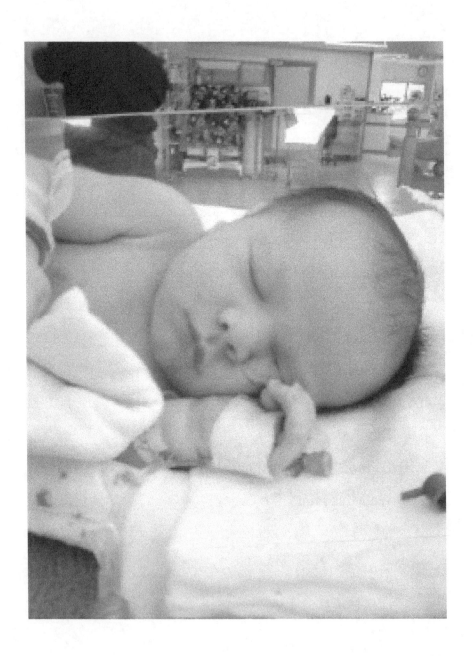

Preface (by Loni Briner)

I was pregnant with my husband's and my first child, Gideon. God had instilled the name "Gideon" on my heart two years prior. I had no idea how meaningful my first-born son's name would become. My husband Harrison and I always thought of Gideon as the Rambo of the Bible- knowing what a warrior the original Gideon was. I never knew how much a warrior our own Gideon would be.

On February 23, 2010 we had our regular 37 week ultrasound. Most doctors don't routinely have a 37 week ultrasound, but ours did. This one seemed to take so much longer than our 21 week ultrasound. The ultrasound technician looked at Gideon for about an hour- which seemed to us to be an unusually long time. As such, Harrison and I began asking the ultrasound technician if something was wrong. She insisted that everything was fine; she just needed some more pictures. She kept looking at his heart. From what we could see, we thought everything looked really strong, of course we weren't experts. Immediately following the ultrasound, we headed for the doctor's office. He would tell us all the results.

The doctor didn't even do an examination on me. He just told us that we had to switch to another (nearby) hospital, one that has many heart specialists for babies/ infants. There they could do an ECHO on

Gideon's heart to see exactly what was wrong. This was because the lady who was doing the ultrasound said that she couldn't get a good image of his heart. We tried to keep calm. I kept telling myself, they are just being safer rather than sorry. My doctor forwarded my medical information to the other hospital and I anxiously awaited a call.

A couple of days later the new hospital called and told me that the only times they could give me an ECHO appointment would be in the middle of my busiest work day. I didn't want to leave work if it was just a precautionary measure. So, meanwhile, I set up a second ultrasound with my original doctor for the day before Gideon's ECHO visit.

On March 2, 2010 we went to my OBGYN's favorite ultrasound technician; earlier my doctor told me, "If this guy likes what he sees, I feel comfortable enough to cancel the echo." My mother, Kim, went with me to this appointment as Harrison had to work. We went in, the ultrasound tech looked for about two minutes, handed me some pictures, gave me a letter for my doctor, and then sent me on my way. We were told to go directly to my doctor. As mom drove, I couldn't help but peek at the letter. It was then that I saw the words that have haunted me ever since: "POSSIBLE DEFECT IN LEFT VENTRICLE."

March 3, 2010 was the date of Gideon's echo. Thankfully Harrison didn't have to work, so he went along with me. This appointment translated to about 3 hours of lots of pressure, as they poked and searched for all of the different pictures and recordings they needed of Gideon's heart. As painful as it was, I knew it needed to be done, and kept telling them to do whatever they needed to do. I just wanted so badly for everything to come back normal. During the course of my visit, I decided to use the bathroom, and from there I heard the ECHO technician ask Harrison, "Is there a history of Congenital Heart Disease in either side of your family?" Harrison said, "No- on both accounts."

Once the technicians were finished, they asked why our doctor elected to do an ultrasound so late, and that normally such was not routine. They said having the 37 week ultrasound and finding this out gave Gideon a chance at life, because they now knew he had Hypoplastic Left Heart Syndrome.

We had no idea how to handle this news, other than lots and lots and lots of prayer. Friends of mine were on a mission trip to Nicaragua, where an entire tribe was praying for our son. Also, one of my mom's old girl scout girls made a facebook page called "Prayers for Gideon." I guess you could say this was where Gideon's ministry really took flight.

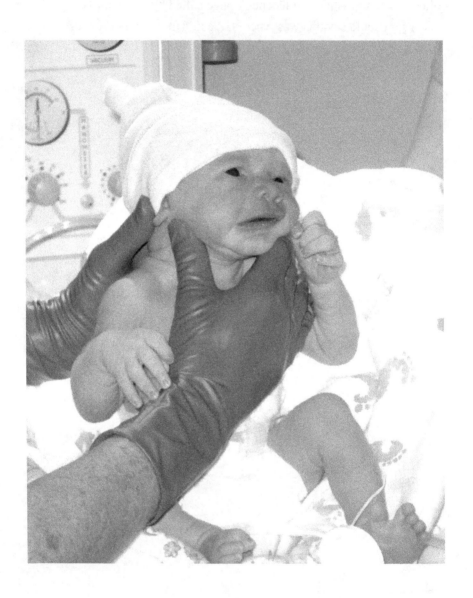

Ch. 1: The Arrival of Gideon (by Harrison Briner)

On the 4th day of March, around 11:30 p.m., Loni began to have frequent contractions. Not paying much attention to her steady whining, I decided to go to sleep. Around 3:30 a.m., my day began with a bang. My wife said her contractions had not subsided at all, but were getting more frequent and worse. I told her to call her mother, who had 6 children of her own, in order to get a professional opinion (so to speak). She told us to get our bag ready; she would be over because we needed to get to the hospital.

We arrived at the hospital around 5:15 a.m. and my wife was in apparent pain. The hosptial had notified our "team" we had arrived and may have a baby soon. The first doctor came in around 5:45 a.m. He made a bold and very wrong prediction saying we would have the baby by that evening (4 p.m. or so). Stuck in a triage room for the next 9 hours, my mother in-law and I decided to take turns sitting with my wife. Since they only allowed one person in the room with her at a time, we didn't have much choice.

The next doctor came in around 10 a.m. and Loni was only dilated 2 centimeters. That poor, poor, doctor had made the mistake of telling my wife she would be admitted and no longer allowed to eat. My wife basically told her, "That's not going to happen." At that point, they came to the compromise that Loni should walk around to help the labor move along- and while she was out she could get something light to eat.

We explored the hospital for a little while, walking up and down the hallways. Eventually we decided just to eat in the "café" that was close to labor and delivery. Around noon, we got back to labor and delivery. At that point we were put right back in the triage room.

For the next 2 hours or so we sat around until a hesitant but intelligent doctor came in and checked Loni's progress. Seeing she had not dilated any further, he reluctantly said we could leave but it would not be smart to go the entire way home. With traffic, home was an hour or so away and our baby definitely needed to be delivered in the hospital. We said we would be 25 minutes away at my wife's sister, Lindsay's home. This pleased the doctor enough to let us leave. Packing up our things, we got out of there before he changed his mind.

On our way to Lindsay's house, Loni decided she wanted to stop in at the office where she works. Her co-workers were having a birthday party and were eager to serve us all lunch. Loni's boss, Jeb, was nervous the entire time we were there, and he cringed with every contraction. We ate and mingled, and Loni insisted on doing a little work. Then we were on our way.

We arrived at Lindsay's around 2:30 in the afternoon. In true "Lindsay fashion," my sister in-law made something for us to eat. Loni decided to walk around first and I was back in the role of Loni stand. Every time she had a contraction she would lean over and hang on me like I was a tree. I would not have volunteered for that job had I known we had 24 hours plus to go. We spent the next 25 min walking, talking, and leaning. Then she decided it was break time, so we went inside and sat around.

Loni sat, laid and tried to get comfortable for what seemed like hours. Around 6 p.m. we sat down and ate a little bit, which was nice. That being said, neither of us ate much- with me being nervous and Loni being in pain. After we ate, my mother and sisters in-law convinced Loni she would feel better if she got a shower. They were right- she seemed rejuvenated when she came out approximately 45 minutes later.

We continued to lay around for the next few hours and around 9 p.m. Loni's contractions got a lot worse and we decided to head back to the hospital. Again, we gathered everything we thought we needed and were about to head out when Loni got sick. (So much for not being stuck in the hospital where she couldn't eat, huh?)

We arrived at the hospital around 10 p.m., 6 hours after first doctor's prediction. Again we were greeted with the triage room of doom but not for long. Around 45 minutes after we arrived my wife was officially admitted to the hospital. Over just about the next 17 hours it was more of the same- getting my hand crushed slowly, walking around, and being a tree. It was just a slow, slow, labor process.

Loni was checked periodically throughout the night, but little progress was made. She was checked around 2 a.m. and was at 6 centimeters, which gave us hope that maybe in the next few hours we would have our baby boy. We were told that a doctor would be in around 6:30 a.m. for shift change; we were very optimistic about the progress that had been made and hoped to be just about there by 6:30 a.m. When no doctor showed at 6:30, then 7:30, then 8:30, I began to get a little angry and my patience was wearing thin.

The doctor finally came in at around nine thirty in the morning and checked Loni for any progress. There was none. Still hanging at 6 centimeters, we were so close, yet so far away. For the next five and a half hours we waited and Loni began to nap in-between contractions as they were getting farther and farther apart. At 2:45 p.m. or so, her contractions were around 7 minutes apart but beginning to worsen- and they did so for the next hour.

Finally, around 3:30 p.m. on the 6th of March, the shift changed and a super-nurse came in roaring.

She came in and asked "how are ya feeling?" then she took one look at Loni and said, "I think we should check you out." She walked over, got a glove, lubed her up, and went to work. She came out with a smile saying, "You're at 10 centimeters and I can feel the head." Rather than listening to the nurse and starting to push, my wife refused for the next few minutes until the doctors had arrived.

The doctor got to the room around 3:45 and my wife began to push. About eight minutes later I saw something kind of "shoot out." It was Gideon's little head, full of hair. Two more big pushes and we had a baby boy at 3:54 p.m. on the 6th day of March 2010, weighing six pounds, two ounces and measuring 20.5 inches long.

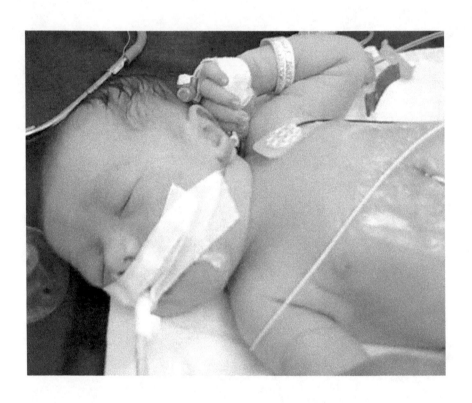

Ch. 2: A Rough First Day

Gideon scored an eight out of ten on his first minute of life, as a part of the APGAR test. He then scored a nine out of ten on the first five minutes for the APGAR test. Everything was looking great. We did not get to hold him because they rushed him off to the Neonatal Infant Care Unit (NICU), which was right down the hall.

They later told us that once they got him down there, his duct above the left ventricle had already closed. On average this duct takes more than a week to close after birth. We aren't completely positive of all the specifications of that process but we do know that until the baby is born and starts to take in air, the duct will stay open as it is in the womb (since babies don't breathe in air while in the womb). After the baby is born and the lungs inflate, the duct closes as it is no longer needed in normal circumstances.

Gideon's situation was far from normal, which made the duct staying open vital for his survival. This process, which normally takes days to weeks, only took minutes for Gideon. Gideon was immediately hooked up to the Prostaglandin (the medicine that keeps that duct open) which didn't just keep the duct open, but saved his life.

Thank God!

One of the many doctors who had been working with Gideon came in to deliver this news and then explained how it was so important that we were at that hospital. If we had not switched hospitals, found out about his out heart defect, and delivered Gideon there, he would not have lived past the point of his duct closing (which was only minutes after birth). If we had stayed with our original hospital that didn't know about Gideon's condition, they would have immediately hooked oxygen up to him. With Hypoplastic Left Heart, that would have filled his lungs with blood, and he would have died instantly.

The next morning there were many tests run on Gideon to see how his heart was doing. They found that his heart's left ventricle was more developed than they previously believed, meaning Gideon's left side didn't stop growing until later in the pregnancy. This meant that this would have been impossible to find until 35 weeks on; making Gideon even more of a miracle.

They found that there was a lack of communication between the atriums, the two upper chambers of his heart. Gideon needed a good hole in between them. This would allow the right side of his heart make up for the work the left side couldn't do. Gideon's hole in the septum between his 2 ventricles was only the size of a pin-hole. That made for a lot of pressure build-up that caused the septum to protrude into the right. Not only was it causing pressure in his heart but also on his lungs. There was too much blood being pushed to the lungs and not being re-turned to the body. The combined amount of pressure in the lungs and heart made surgery an immediate necessity.

Gideon was only 23 hours old when they sent him for his first sur-gery. Talking amongst themselves, the cardiologists, along with Gideon's future heart surgeon, agreed that a catheterization surgery would be best in this situation. Assuring us Gideon would have a lot less trauma to his body this way, they explained to us what needed to be accomplished and how they were going to do it.

They would take a tiny catheter (with a wire on the end) up through his leg and into Gideon's right ventricle. Using microwaves they would heat the wire end up and burn a hole in the septum. Then they would blow up a balloon and pull it through the new hole and make it big enough to sustain blood flow between the two ventricles- this would carry him through until his first big surgery. We were told this would be a temporary- but necessary fix.

Everything went well, except they hit the back of Gideon's heart, and made a small hole there. It bled a bit, but healed quickly. So for the next few days he needed a drainage tube out of his chest to drain any blood and fluids from his chest cavity. This surgery also caused a clot to form in this right leg, where the catheter went in. So Gideon was put on blood thinners for the next week or so to help remove the clot.

All in all things started looking up. We were so glad that the first surgery went well and were incredibly happy to have him for the next few days. Praise God for sharing his wisdom with men and directing them in the ways of modern medicine.

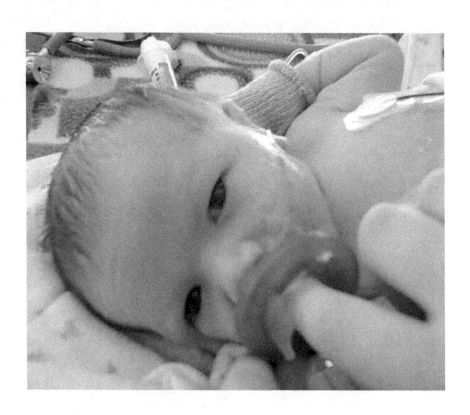

Ch. 3: Lots of Love

Throughout Gideon's hospital stay he had many, many visitors. From his grandparents to great-grandparents, from aunts and uncles to great aunts and uncles, and from our pastor to friends of the family- there seemed to be someone by Gideon's side all the time. But we also got to spend a lot of just "parents and baby time" with him.

It was in our alone time that we really got to know him and find out how much we loved everything about him. He had his daddy's curly hair, his mommy's mouth, and the biggest feet that we'd ever seen on a baby. His long legs were a gift from God because Mommy and Daddy definitely didn't have anything to do with them. He was so attentive, and loved shiny things. He seemed to be looking around an awful lot. We have to believe that he could see the angels that God had surround- ing his bedside.

Just like his daddy, Gideon loved it when he was getting his head rubbed. He would sometimes just close his eyes, as if he were saying, "That's the spot, right there."

Throughout the pregnancy he often heard us trying to get our noisy cockatiel to be quiet. The same noises that usually worked for the bird, also worked for Gideon. Of course he recognized those sounds that he had often heard while in the womb. The same was true with his mom's voice and his father's voice- especially when Harrison would say Gideon's name long and low. Not only was it soothing to Gideon, but it was familiar. He knew without a doubt his dad was there when he heard his voice.

Something else that Gideon learned to associate with us was his "binky". Even though we don't agree with the practice of the use of the bink in our house, Gideon was an exception. We felt it was OK for Gideon to use a binky since he was never allowed to eat orally. All his nutrition was fed intravenously. He was given many things everyday including: saline solution (salt water), lipids, and his other necessary nourishments. The nurses were too busy to sit by his side all of the time, so they would just give him his bink and carry on. We would hold it and let him gnaw on our fingers and make the binky more of an enjoyable experience.

After days of life and having no food, you can imagine that he was a hungry little man. The nurses would keep a syringe of diluted sugar water (Neosweet) by his side. When Gideon would get really hungry they would drop a small amount of it into his mouth to give him the sensation that he was eating. The fluid dissolved before hitting his stomach, so it was pretty safe. Gideon sure did love that Neosweet.

Gideon was the cutest baby that we have ever seen. He had a cute little button nose, chubby cheeks, and a whole lot of hair! He was just like his parents in that he was a roochy, roochy sleeper. When he would sleep he would be so relaxed that his mouth just dropped. There wasn't a sleeping position that he didn't love. He loved his back because he could stretch out; he loved his belly because it was all nice and cozy; and he loved his side because he had a good view of things around him.

Every time Gideon would open his eyes, we would just melt. He had such big, beautiful, loving eyes. Everyone who got to meet him could see just how gorgeous and perfect he was. Not only was he gorgeous, but he was ours. For 13 wonderful days, he was ours.

When Harrison ran home for clothing, it was just mommy and aunt Lainey left to sit with Gideon. For the 3 hour trip, Gideon tried so hard to wait for Harrison. He tried and tried and tried to keep himself awake long enough for his daddy to get back. With heavy eyes he fought and about ten minutes before Harrison got there, he couldn't fight the tiredness anymore and fell asleep. It was so cute.

Because of all of the wires and tubes hooked up to Gideon, we were not allowed to hold him. This was also the reason that he was not allowed to be nursed (he couldn't be burped). For a baby that couldn't be held, couldn't eat, and couldn't move freely, Gideon was very well behaved.

Not only was Gideon getting lots of love, but there were many sources showing us God's love. Once discharged from the hospital we ran across the parking lot to the "Ronny House" to try to get a room. We really needed this room so that we could be close to Gideon. They filled the only available room from the time that we checked out and crossed the parking lot. But later that day one of Gideon's surgeon's assistants had called over and the house had an opening. One more run there and we were in.

Again, thank God!

The Ronny House was so helpful and supportive. They understood and provided sources we needed throughout our stay and Gideon's hospital stay. The best part was that we could go to sleep at night, knowing that we were so close to our baby and that if they needed us, we were only a parking lot away.

When Gideon was taken to the NICU, we made sure he had a Bible by his bed and everyday we would read it to Gideon. Sometimes we would just open the Bible to a bunch of spots and just read. One day we caught a verse that summed up what Gideon was going through perfectly. Psalm 73:26 (NKJV) reads: "My flesh and my heart fail; *But* God *is* the strength of my heart and my portion forever."

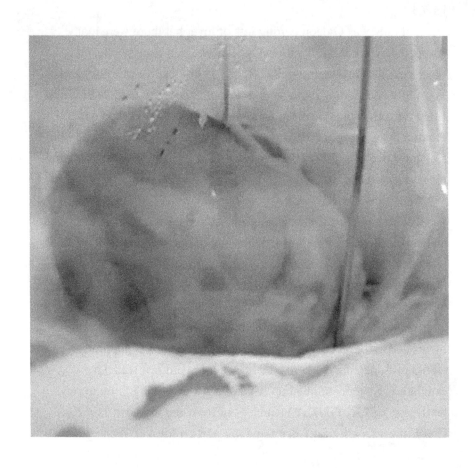

Ch. 4: The Baby in the Bubble

On March 11th we had lunch with Gideon's Uncle David. When we were allowed back into see him, there was a very unpleasant surprise. Gideon was stuck in a plastic hood from his shoulders up. Mommy was especially unhappy about this. We thought we could no longer rub his head, or hold his hand, or even give him his bink. We quickly learned our way around this obstacle. As long as we kept the plastic hood as tight as possible, we could maneuver inside that bubble.

Of course Gideon was not always fond of the hood himself. It got really hot and it formed a lot of condensation on the inside, so his hair was wet the whole time he was in it. They eventually had to turn his heat lamp off, because it made him so hot. We looked at him and thought it was like he had his own baby sauna. Then across the room, the preemies under the fluorescent lights looked like they had their own tanning booths. The NICU looked like a baby spa.

We kept asking everyone if they could get him a bigger bubble, it looked so tight on him. The respiratory people just told us that they normally use smaller bubbles than the one he had; and that they were be able to control Gideon's air easier with that small of a bubble. After at least eight hours of the "stupid hood," one of the respiratory nurses looked at the box and said, "Oh," and then punched in the hole on the top of the plastic. By this point, it was so steamed up that you could not see Gideon in there. It cleared up pretty quickly once that hole was opened.

As shocked and angry as we were to see the bubble, after speaking to the cardiologist we learned that it was a necessary evil. This oxygen hood kept the oxygen level in the air that Gideon was breathing at 17 to 18 percent. Normal room air (which he had been breathing since day one) is 21 percent. This inconvenience for us would help clear his lungs up and keep his lungs from getting over saturated with blood. This is what they used to help get his lungs ready for surgery.

For the first day Gideon absolutely hated the hood. It was like he was claustrophobic. He was continually pushing and punching on it. But one afternoon when we went into see him, he had his face smashed up against the side of the bubble. He was really comfortable- even with his self-inflicted piggy nose.

The day that they put the hood over Gideon, he had a group of visitors. Some of his great-aunts came in to see him for the first time, and his mom was mad. Gideon's uncle Ben was not able to see Gideon until after the hood was on, as well. He waited to get over a cold, so that he wouldn't bring any germs into the NICU. But luckily for him, when he came in, it was the same time they were doing a neuron-echo on Gideon's head and Ben was there to see Gideon out of the hood. Gideon loved the head scan, it was nothing but rubbing a roller across his head, and he really liked that.

We found out that it is more common for a baby with Hypoplastic Left Heart Syndrome to be placed directly into a bubble after birth. For the next five days, we watched our baby boy through a plastic bubble. Even though we were upset about the bubble, we felt spoiled that we had the first five days without the bubble. We thank God for every second that we got to have with him, bubble or no bubble.

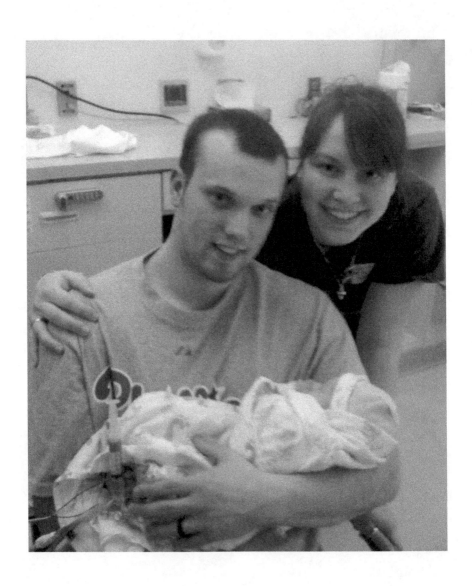

Ch. 5: For the First Time

For nine days we were not able to hold our baby. It was too danger-ous to chance any of his medicine lines being compromised. We held his hand, rubbed his head, and comforted him in any way that we could without picking him up. It was very difficult not to snatch him up and cradle him in our arms whenever he would cry, or fuss in general. Diffi-cult probably isn't even the word for not being able to comfort your child. In fact, being forced to have such limited contact with our baby was more like a bad nightmare.

The whole time we were told that we would get to hold him the morning of his surgery. But the nurse who was on the night before thought it would be best to hold him that night. That way it couldn't get too busy and chance us not being able to hold him at all. So as soon as Harrison got back from work he jumped in the shower, and we ran across the parking lot to see Gideon. We got there around 10:45 p.m. and the nurse had him all swaddled and ready for us.

Since he was out of his bubble, they had breathing tubes up his nose. This he did not like at all. We had found out many times earlier anything in his nose or mouth would not be tolerated or taken lightly. Gideon had to be sedated after his first catheterization surgery because he was trying to rip his breathing tube out of his mouth. He also pulled out a small tube that was very uncomfortably placed down his nose (to keep air bubbles from forming in his stomach) and he held it like a trophy for all to see.

Mommy held him first. The tubes kept falling out of his nose, so it was easiest to give him his binky to hold them in. There were also the syringes that they used to do Gideon's blood work; we had to hold them up so that his IV wouldn't rip out. He sat there and looked around and looked at his mom and looked around some more. It had to be exciting to see all the new sights (even if they were only two feet from where he normally laid). After about 15 to 20 minutes the nurse came back and it was daddy's turn. Of course he fell asleep just before the baby-handoff. Daddy got to hold him for about the same amount of time, only Gideon was so tired, he slept through it.

Gideon was so precious. Embracing him was our "dream come true." It was nice to hold him. It was all that we wanted to do since the moment he was born. It stank having all the wires and hook-ups there, but at least we got to hold him. It felt so natural holding our little man of valor close to us. Our embrace was something that so many take for granted, and if we had known what was to come we probably would have never let him go.

Normally we would have gotten kicked out of the NICU at 11:00 p.m., but we didn't leave until 12:30 a.m. They were understanding and supportive. After holding him, we helped to settle him back into his bed and spent some more quality time with him. We had to be up in four hours to meet Lindsay's pastor, so even though we wanted to, we couldn't stay all night. It wasn't easy to get to sleep but we both did. Neither of us thought of anything but the best outcome and we were very optimistic about the coming day's events. God's love had pulled us through the last few days and we were sure going to need him in the days to come.

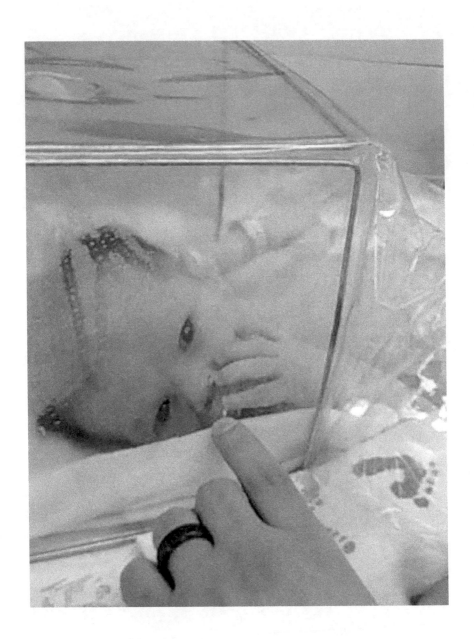

Ch. 6: Surgery Day

We were up early on the 16th of March, both nervous and hopeful. As we walked across the parking lot to meet Lindsay's pastor at 5:15 a.m., we were holding hands and just relying on one another but mostly on God. We sat down and discussed some of the Bible but just generally got to know a strong man of faith. Talking about ourselves and our situation, we had a new strength of hope.

Not wishing to be rude by being relieved when we parted with the pastor early that morning, we hurried up to our baby- not wanting to be away from him for a minute more. No one except God knew what would unfold that day. We were nervous and anxious to say the least. We sat with Gideon for a while not wanting to wake him, and to just allowed Gideon to rest, knowing he had a long day ahead.

We sat for a while and waited thinking that our 7:30 a.m. start time was on schedule. 7:30 quickly became 8:00 and daddy's patience was starting to wear thin. Not very accepting when things aren't exactly on time, he was starting to pace and get upset. Five minutes later the anesthesiologists walked into the NICU and no sooner did they get there than Gideon became hysterical.

No one had touched Gideon, or done anything yet, so we were a little concerned as to why he would be crying. They were about to move Gideon to the surgical room when they got a call from the surgeon who was both a blessing and a perfectionist. Apparently everything wasn't perfectly set up and the anesthesiologists told us it would be another 15-20 minutes until they'd get the show on the road. Not long after they walked away, Gideon stopped crying and went back to sleep.

20 minutes ended up being 40 minutes and daddy was not happy. We were an hour and ten minutes behind schedule and this was not at all "ok" in his eyes. As soon as the anesthesiologists returned, so did Gideon's screaming. Later we discussed why Gideon was so upset and Loni said that Gideon had known what was going to happen. It was his way of showing us he didn't want to leave us, but it was God's plan for him.

We walked with the team as they escorted our son into surgery. He didn't stop crying the entire way. After we got there, we kissed him and said we would see him later and to be strong through the surgery. Then we both broke down a little bit. We stood in the hall for a while, crying and holding each other. Knowing we had folks waiting for us in the NICU waiting room, we pulled it together and headed that way.

From this point forward Gideon taught us a big lesson on patience.

The rest of the day was very relaxed. We talked and ate and just tried to find things to do while we waited. It wasn't easy keeping it together knowing our son's life was in the hands of someone other than mom and dad. It's a surreal feeling not being able to help your son through such a tough event. The fact that our son was just ten days old didn't help either. But all of our friends and family were helping time pass quickly, and keeping us preoccupied.

Gideon's surgeon told us to wait until the evening to come to the waiting room and that we should count on surgery taking all day (even if it were best case scenario). So we found our way to a new waiting room, this time for the Pediatric Intensive Care Unit (PICU). This is where they were taking our son after his surgery. We got there at 5:00 p.m. and let them know we were there and waiting.

15 minutes later a nurse came out and told us that they were getting ready to bring Gideon down, but things weren't looking good. She

didn't know any details, but they informed the PICU that he was not yet stable and that he was losing a lot of blood. She would let us know as soon as they knew more. We really appreciated how honest everyone at the hospital was, and the fact they never sugar-coated anything.

We all gathered, for the first time together, and prayed. Moments later they flew past our window, with our son still in the same bed that he had spent his entire life. The nurse came out a little while later and said that things weren't as bad as she thought they were. They were still trying to stabilize Gideon, but things seemed hopeful.

Hours passed and no word. Around 10:00 p.m. the surgeon came out to the waiting room and rushed us into the hallway to talk to us alone. He said Gideon was still not stable and they were beginning to look at other options. "Gideon's heart is really tired and not calming down." He was still losing an enormous amount of blood. He said that they weren't giving up and he would have "the talk" with us if he felt they would ever need to. Now was not that time. (The surgeon was completely honest about everything throughout this complete ordeal, which we really appreciated.) He wanted to get back in with Gideon immediately, so he kept it short.

The next two hours was nothing but prayer between us and our visitors. Many phone calls were made, and so the prayers kept spreading. At midnight they called us back to a consulting room, across from the room that Gideon was in, to wait for the doctor. He wanted to talk with us.

All we thought was that we were about to have "the talk" with him. Both of us were a nervous wreck. But when the doctor came in, we tried to stay as calm as possible.

When the surgeon came in he said what they were doing wasn't working and that there was only one last ditch-effort they had to attempt. He wasn't sure if it would work and that it was risky. They wanted to rest Gideon's heart by hooking up a heart/lung machine (ECMO) so it could do the work instead of Gideon. Once on this machine, however, they could not leave him on for more than a few days because his body would become dependent. We said, "Whatever it takes, do it." We trusted the surgeon's opinion and trusted him.

They wanted us to go in and say our "good-byes," for fear that this procedure wouldn't work. We went in, kissed him and we asked him to keep fighting. We didn't want to say good-bye; we wanted him to get through this so we could take him home and watch him grow.

At 1:00 a.m. the doctor told us that they successfully put Gideon on the machine and he was finally stable. The doctor was going to try to sleep a bit before the next day's work. We informed our people and went in to see our son.

Before we could even begin to think about sleep we wanted to see what kind of people were going to be working with our son all night. We were pleased knowing that one of the surgeon's assistants was with Gideon, along with two other nurses and three men running the heart/ lung machine. There was always at least one of them watching the ECMO, putting us at an ease.

Setting in the window beside Gideon's bed was a picture of Jesus holding a baby. This was soothing and uplifting. To turn to that image was encouraging- reminding us that no matter what the future was going to bring, Gideon was in God's hands.

We kissed our baby, held his hand, said our prayers with Gideon and set off for a nap before the morning. The next day was supposed to give us a better idea of what to expect. We had faith and high hopes. Only time would tell what God's plans were.

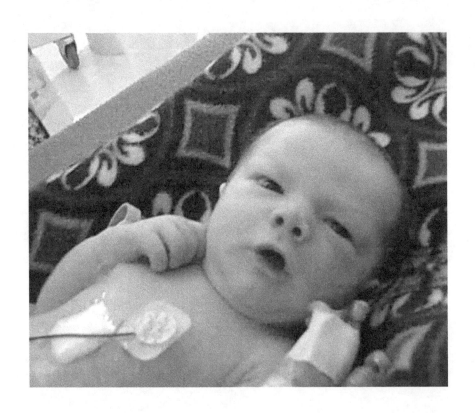

Ch. 7: A Good Day

We woke around 8:00 a.m. on March 17th and immediately called the PICU for a progress report with great expectations. They really had no news. We hurriedly showered and brushed our teeth wanting to get over to see Gideon and find our more about what the night had brought.

His surgeon was there when we got there. He said that Gideon's acid levels were off the chart, which was a bad sign. These levels told us how well Gideon's body was accepting its oxygen. We wanted a level of one or two, but Gideon's was above 30. They couldn't tell how high above 30 because that is as high as a person can measure. This was a big part of our prayers that day- continued prayer that Gideon's body would begin to accept its oxygen.

Our parents showed up around 10am. Nana and Pappy Briner brought some donuts while Grammy and Pappy Martz brought subs, trying to get us to eat. By 4pm that afternoon, our fan base was there in full charge again. For a room that sat eight people, we loaded it with at least 18 at a shot. Lots of people were in and out of the visiting room all evening. Countless times we would all bow to pray, often in a joint circle. We turned that tiny room into our own little sanctuary.

Throughout the day, some of Gideon's different nurses from the NICU would stop down to ask us how he was doing, as did some parents of other babies who we also met at the NICU. His nurses, however, had grown attached to our little angel, and were especially concerned.

With Gideon sitting back in the PICU recovery room, we were allowed to see him whenever we wanted. Technically, we could have taken one person back at a time but we didn't want others seeing him in that condition. While Gideon's mommy wanted to stay by his side every second, both mom and dad knew that the doctors needed to do what they needed to do.

Every time we were with him, some type of alarm would sound and we would need to move out of the way to let the nurses change a medicine, or reset a computer of some type. He did, after all, have different meds that lined up from the floor to the ceiling. We wanted them to be able to do what they had to for our baby with ease, so we only made short visits every now and then, spending the rest of our time out with our "guests."

The surgeon kept Gideon's chest open to have easy access to keep the swelling down, to have the ECMO hooked up, and in case they needed to do any surgical procedures. Therefore, they had to keep Gideon from being the roochy baby that he was. They didn't want to keep him under anesthesia, so every time he began to move, they would give him a drug to paralyze him and keep him comfortable at the same time.

Gideon had become very swollen everywhere, especially the face. They told us that because of this, he would not be able to open his eyes. But Gideon showed them!

Whenever we would come around daddy would say, deep and slow, "Gideon" and he heard him, as well as his mommy's voice. Gideon let us know he heard us. He started opening his big, beautiful eyes and looked right at us. He squeezed our hands and starting making a face like he was sucking on a binky. These became some of the best moments we had with our son. The fact that he communicated so clearly with us, fighting the paralyzing drugs, was just amazing. We can say with absolutely no doubt our son loved us. He really, truly loved us.

As we talked to him, we told him how great he was doing- how proud we were of him. And we told him how much we would appreciate it if he could just keep fighting. We told him that we couldn't wait to take him home. We also reminded him that mommy had been saving lots of milk for him and that he needed to get better so that he could finally have his first meal.

We continued to read Gideon's Bible to him each day and to pray with him. The technical people and nurses were shocked to see that. I guess they would have expected us to turn from God and blame Him for the circumstances. We couldn't do that, though. God was the only one who could bring Gideon out of this, if it had been his plan. We had no control in any of this. All we could do was surrender to the maker who blessed us with a baby, for finding the problem, giving us all of those moments, keeping us strong through it all.

It was amazing to see that tiny little body, fighting enough meds to paralyze an adult, showing us how much he loved us and wanted us. But because he was so excited with us around, we could not stay with him. They did not want to have to keep pumping those drugs into him. The hardest thing we've ever done was leave Gideon's side through this. But we had to. If we wanted to see him get better, we had to.

At 4:00 p.m. we finally saw the light at the end of the tunnel, with an acid level of 29. Yes, this number was still horrible, but it was better than off the charts.

As always, thank God!

We persisted with our prayers and by 8:00 p.m. the levels were down to 22! Things were looking really good. Still, we prayed, and at midnight the acid level came down even more to 20. We were so happy. We could have another good night of rest.

We rested peacefully too soon. At 6:30 a.m. the next morning we received the phone call that changed our lives forever.

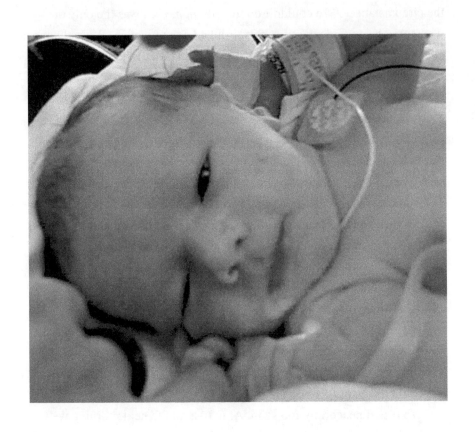

Ch. 8: Red Baby

We were abruptly awakened on the 18th of March from our single beds. Before daddy could figure out what the noise was, mommy had already answered the phone. As with most situations like this, when a doctor says he needs time "no news is good news." Our phone was ringing at 6:30 in the morning so this couldn't be good news; we quickly found that it wasn't.

Sometime around 6 a.m. the ECMO machine had clotted. For about three minutes Gideon had no blood or oxygen to his precious little body. When this happens to the body, especially in such a traumatized state, Gideon's body constricted. Every vein, blood vessel, and capillary in Gideon's body tightened. It took three minutes to replace the machine's piece, and that was why it took so long to get things back up and running.

By the time we got over there the doctors had stabilized him as best they could and started treating this new situation. He was on massive doses of drugs to dilate his veins and blood vessels. It would be slow going and again, the surgeon asked us for time.

Our baby no longer looked like a baby at all. Gideon's entire body was beet red and we could see all of the spots where the veins and vessels had not re-opened. The veins and vessels were dark purple and stuck out in his overall red color. They also had his eyes covered because they could not get him to keep his eyes closed. It was very hard to see our baby in this condition after having such a good day the day before.

We were shocked, upset, and sad, but even though we had these brief moments of emotion we looked to the Lord for help and He answered. Our family started pouring in from the news they received that morning. We had pastors and friends and people we didn't even know stopping in to pray both with and for us.

We were told by the surgeon we were far beyond being back at square one. We were in a much worse state now than before and the only thing we could do was attack it "with both guns blazing". This reaffirmed our already strong feelings of admiration for this man. Only God could put the perfect man in the perfect job like this. His absolute loyalty to his patients and "never say die" attitude gave us great hope throughout the entire struggle. Not once did he fill us with false hope or beat around the bush. He was always very clear on the dangers of every situation.

One great report through all of this was that Gideon's brain activity was as perfect as always and that we hadn't lost him at all up there.

By around noon a slew of family and friends were sitting in with us. We went back to check on Gideon and there wasn't much change for the better. He hadn't fallen back any farther though, either.

His body was still very acidotic (meaning the acidosis was worse then before), and his veins and vessels were still closed. It was mostly in his fingers and toes, but also his entire right leg (where his blood clot was after the first surgery). Gideon's surgeon told us he had almost completely removed the line from the leg to see if it would help the blood flow. So far it had not and he was getting very skeptical about whether or not it would. He said he was going to continue what he was doing that we should try to get something to eat and come back later as he needed time. So that's what we did.

When we went back to the room we gave everyone a situation report and then (as usual) we all bowed our heads in prayer. We prayed for Gideon's health and strength and focused mostly on the things the surgeon said needed to change.

By late afternoon we were back in the PICU with our son and wanting news. His body's veins and vessels were beginning to dilate more and more. His outer extremities and his right leg were not dilated yet though. Again we heard the doctors were attacking with both guns blazing and that the acidosis had subsided some (not nearly to the point it needed to) but there was some progress, none the less.

The rest of the day we sat with family and friends praying, talking, crying, and holding one another. No one knew what was going to happen. By that point God had everyone in that room believing in and praying for a miracle.

Later that night our surgeon came to the waiting room and spoke with us about the little progress he had seen and that he wanted to take another night to see if any more progress would be made. He wanted to know if there was anything that we, as Gideon's parents, needed. All we wanted to do was to pray for this amazing doctor. He had no objections, so we did. Our mothers later told us that a man was looking at us praying as he walked by and almost slammed his face into the corner-wall.

We went in to see Gideon directly after speaking to the surgeon. The new doctor on call told us to go to our room at the "Ronny House" and try to get some rest and that if at any point she felt like they were "doing stuff to our baby instead of for him" she would call us and let us know.

Reluctantly, we left Gideon's bedside after praying over him and saying his prayers with him as we did every night of his life. We prayed over the new doctor (putting us at ease) and headed on our way. Arriving back to the waiting room we told everyone the news and that they could go home. We prayed for Gideon and for safe travels for our guests. We went back to the room exhausted. We were emotionally and physically drained from the last 12 days. It took a while, but eventually we both passed out. Still hopeful and trusting in God's purpose, we slept.

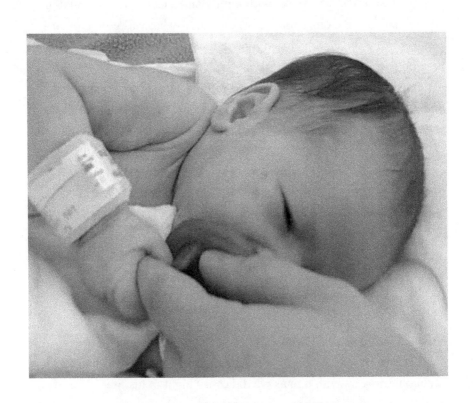

Ch. 9: Day 13

We slept like rocks that night despite our son's life hanging in the balance. Showered and ready to head over to the hospital, the phone rang. The last time our phone rang it was because the ECMO machine had clotted and shut down so we knew this couldn't be good. Our surgeon's assistant was on the phone and said we needed to get over there; our surgeon wanted to talk to us. This couldn't be good and we knew it.

Weary and afraid, we made the trek across the parking lot to the children's wing and then to the PICU. Once there, they sat us down in the same room where they told us they would be giving their last ditch effort and putting Gideon on the ECMO machine. Our surgeon and the female doctor from the night before were in directly and told us it was time to have "the talk" that we were dreading to have.

They were no longer doing things for our son they were only doing things to him. The surgeon told us that they would be taking Gideon off the ECMO and that he thought Gideon wouldn't last long once off of it. They would be giving him things to make him very comfortable and would see what happened, but our surgeon was not optimistic. He felt the only thing he could do was keep Gideon as comfortable as possible. Also, in order to take Gideon off the machine, they needed to put him under anesthesia.

Our families were all there already. So we went out, told them, and then went back and waited for it to be ok to so see him. We took a few minutes in the small room outside of where Gideon was and cried. It's not like we didn't have this possibility in the back of our heads, but we never thought it would come to this. Still crying a little, we went in to see our son while he was still alive in body one last time.

It almost looked to us that he had been gone for some time, though. Our beautiful baby boy was no longer how we had spent all those wonderful days with him. His chest was opened, and he was red with purple splotches from head to toe. But our son was still there in mind.

We started talking to him and he was giving us his "sucking the bink" face. His mouth started going and his little fingers (that weren't getting any circulation) were going. Under anesthesia, that was miraculous. We talked with him and asked him to show them all and to pull through this, but if he didn't want to it would be ok, we understood. We read to him from his Bible, and we prayed and cried over our son. We said his prayers with him one last time and told him how much we loved him and how much we would miss him. We really wanted to see him fight through this, but if he didn't we knew he would be going to a better place. This didn't make us want him with us any less.

The doctors told us to take our time, just to let them know when we were ready. We didn't want to take up time of doctors who could be saving other babies' lives. Besides, we easily could have sat there all day. So we made our last 20 minutes worth it and tried to stay strong.

We thanked everyone for their efforts and for having such persistence with our son's medical attention. We slowly walked over to the waiting room to tell our friends and families what was going on. We stayed in the room with our guests and we cried and prayed and were leaning on one another for the next hour or so.

Our surgeon came out from the back and told us that after they took Gideon off the ECMO he only lasted a few moments. He let us know that they would get his body sewn up and dressed if we would like to take some time with his body. We said yes and we went back to tell everyone the news and again we cried and held one another.

In this time, we were in and out of the waiting room. When we were in the hallway, our people in the waiting room said the lights had flashed brightly. It was like they had dimmed for a brief moment and then got really bright. (It is great to think that it was a sign of Jesus coming down to take our baby to his everlasting home.)

A short time later, our family case worker came in with one of the spiritual advisors to take us back to see our son. When we got there he was all swaddled and for the first time we got to hold our son with no wires or machines. As hard as it was to know that he wasn't physically there and alive we like to think he was in the room with us, and that God allowed our son to stay and let us feel his presence as we held, and cuddled, and spoke to our son.

It was surreal knowing he wasn't coming home with us, but feeling so close to him. It was so hard- not just for us- but for our families, too. He never met one of his aunts because of her being sick. He also never got to meet one of his uncles because he was unattainable, due to his military services.

We loved our son so much for the short time we had him and we have missed him every second since he passed. Sitting in that small room with all the visitors was almost like what we expected to happen right after he was born. It wasn't supposed to be like this. We were supposed to be taking our baby home-not leaving without him. It took a little while but eventually we were ready to give our son's body back to the hospital.

Our son's spirit was with the Lord and we knew that and took solace in it. Eventually we left but not before the hospital gave us a memorial box that had Gideon's foot and hand prints in it. It also had a certificate of life and some other things like a lock of his hair and pamphlets for grieving parents. They also gave us the blanket that he was wrapped in the night we held him, his wrist and leg bands he had worn since day one, and the blanket he wore when we held him that day. This was in addition to his little hat that he wore the night we held him, that was given to us by the NICU nurse when they took him into surgery. This was great because it still smelled like him.

We went over to the "Ronny House" and packed up while our family and friends cleaned the room for us. After that we did not know where to go or what to do; our world was upside down and has been ever since then. We missed him immediately and still do every second of every day. Driving away from the hospital, we felt like we had forgotten something. We guess that we can count on feeling like something is missing from our lives until we meet Gideon again, someday.

Not all parents get to spend time with their babies, so we thank God for our 13 days with Gideon and wouldn't exchange it for anything.

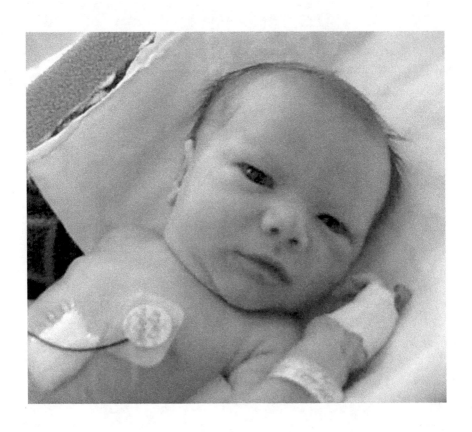

Ch. 10: Gideon's Funeral and Legacy

God blessed us with an understanding funeral director. He didn't charge anything for his funeral costs (something that they do for any infant services). The only cost was Gideon's white-marbled coffin (which was paid for by dear friends of ours). We had a simple, grave-side service at our little country church. We had a couple of framed pictures and a poster board full of pictures of our baby.

There were so many flowers that people bought for Gideon's funeral. Everything was beautiful. The sun was shining and the wind was still. We got the corner-plot, by the field. Gideon was buried in his sweater vest outfit and his John Deere socks. They weren't able to make his body presentable, so it was all closed casket.

There were so many people who came. It was amazing. There were anywhere from 100 to 150 family members, friends, co-workers, and church families. They were all people who came to show comfort and support in our great time of need. Very few people had actually gotten to meet Gideon, but that doesn't even diminish the number of lives that Gideon touched in his brief life.

His facebook group has over 800 people and rising. Our families were keeping people from all over updated about Gideon, his condition, and his struggles. Many people said that Gideon's life brought them closer to God. There were many who admitted that they were pulling away from God, but praying for Gideon brought them back. Some who hadn't prayed in a long time bowed their heads because of him. So many spiritual seeds were planted because of our son. Gideon was a hero. All we can do is be proud of Gideon for all of the lives he touched.

We could not have ever imagined that our two families would be joined spiritually. But for three days straight Gideon did it. He had us joined hand-in-hand in prayer, drawing us closer with his every breath. Gideon was amazing.

One of the verses that we read to Gideon was Jeremiah 1:5a "Before I formed you in the womb I knew you; before you were born I sanctified you;" and we have to believe that this remains true for everyone. Knowing this has comforted and strengthened us, knowing that Gideon sacrificed a long life to help save others. In return, both of us agreed to only having our son for such a short time, in order for his mission to be carried out. Again, we are just so proud of his fight, and of him.

We aren't angry that our son is gone. He is another reason that we can praise God for the sacrifice of His Son, Jesus Christ, and His surrender made on the cross so that we can reunite with Gideon and spend eternity with him.

If things would not have happened the way that they did, days before Gideon was born, we would not have had any time with him. Out of all the many wonderful things that Gideon brought, we have also the 13 days of memories with our gorgeous, wonderful, brave son.

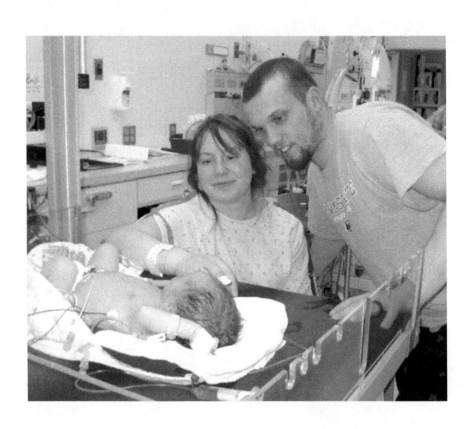

Ch. 11: We Miss Him Like Crazy

<u>Notes from Daddy</u>:

As I drove home on April 25th, which was my first day back to work, I was reflecting on the prior weeks and what they had revealed to me.

On March 6th 2010 I was the happiest man on earth; my son Gideon was born. Through the next 13 days I would find glory in God and His plan. My beautiful baby boy would do more for me in his 13 days than I could of ever have done for him. He brought me closer to God and His glory than anyone else on earth could have. He revealed a faith in me that I never thought I had.

I am so proud and thankful to my son. His struggle brought thousands of believers and non-believers closer to God. Thinking about how beautiful he was when he did anything from kicking his little feet in defiance of someone waking him up, to every little coo and sound he made, my son had me hanging on his every breath.

The ten days before his surgery were the happiest ten days of my life. Watching my son every day and the joy he brought me is unmatched in this world. If the love of a father could have healed his heart, mine would have ten fold. Watching the different times my family was able to come and sit with him were some of the greatest sights I have ever witnessed. Seeing the joy he brought my wife was so beautiful.

I continue to see him in everything and everywhere I go. Little noises or smells bring him back to my mind with an unsurpassed freshness. I miss not getting up in the morning and rushing to his bedside. It pains me greatly we never got to wake me up in the middle of the night to feed him or change his diaper. Things so many new mothers and fathers complain about are the things I never got to experience and would give my right arm to have.

I know he is in a better place and he gets to have an eternity in God's glory, but it still doesn't stop me from wanting him back, not just emotionally because he is here in my heart and will be forever. I wanted to watch my son grow and show him how much I loved him. I wanted to take him out on the tractor when I mowed the lawn. I wanted to teach him how to play ball. I wanted to teach him wrong from right. I just wanted him to be around his daddy.

It's not a natural thing for a father to bury his child. My wife and I had to so early in life and nothing could have prepared us for it. We miss our son every minute of the day. We can only hope and pray that we live a good life in God's eyes and he allows us to come to heaven and be reunited with our son.

Notes from Mommy:

I used to look at life and how much I loved it here and I did not look forward to death. I wasn't afraid of dying; I know where I will go. I just loved what God was doing for me here. Then I met Gideon. I never felt a deeper love in my life. God gave me the most precious gift, even if it was only for a short time. I could not have imagined a more handsome face if I tried. He was so perfectly beautiful.

My husband and I feel so blessed to have had 13 days with our son. Not every parent gets that. There are so many miscarriages and stillborn babies. The way we see it, we were the lucky ones. Do we wish we had our baby to raise? Of course! I wanted to kiss his boo-boos and make them better. I wanted to put him in all the cute little outfits that we got him. I wanted to take him home to his room that we had all ready for him and watch him sleep in his crib. But he is in a better place feeling no pain, and his heart is now perfect and whole. So I am not about to complain.

I really believe that Gideon was getting a tour of Heaven in the minutes that he didn't have blood pumping through his veins. And if I were him, I probably would have picked Heaven too. And I am sure once he got there he ate an amazing first meal, even better than milk.

It is remarkable to consider how big God's love is. I know just how much I love Gideon. To think that God loves his children more than that, meaning He loves Gideon more than I can; I find that amazing. And God holds that same love for me! He was willing to give up His only Son for us. I will admit, when we were with Gideon we were not willing to give him up, however we did not have a choice.

Gideon was the best thing that ever happened to me. I miss him in everything I do. I could very easily sit and cry all day everyday. But it wouldn't change anything. It wouldn't bring my baby back. There wasn't anything that we could have done to keep him on earth with us. It is very obvious that we are not the ones in control.

So what is the use of becoming depressed and weeping all day? Gideon wouldn't want us to act that way. It won't make time pass any faster. And it certainly wouldn't be to God's glory. So all I can try to do now is live a full life pleasing to God until the day He calls me to my real, everlasting home.

Now I see just how much the life of a Christian is a really a win-win situation. I will enjoy my life here to my best ability, to honor Gideon's life. But my days on earth are numbered. I have something even more wonderful to look forward to. Not only will I get to see the face of God, but also the face of my gorgeously, handsome baby. And what a glorious day that will be.

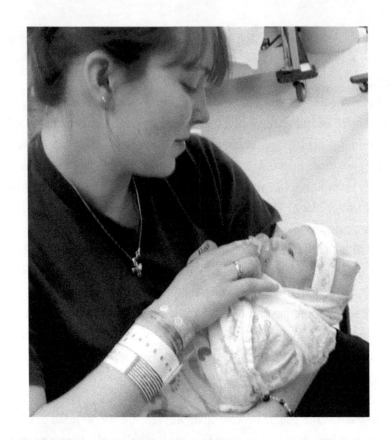

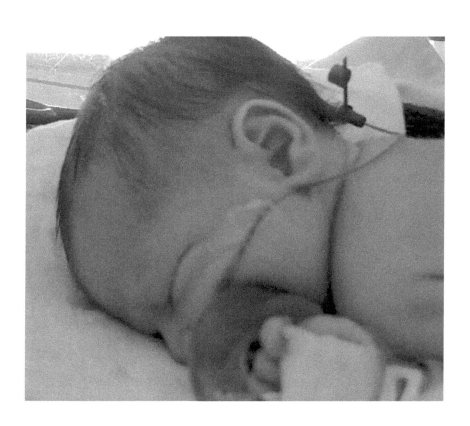

In memory of

Gideon William Briner

March 6, 2010 - March 19, 2010

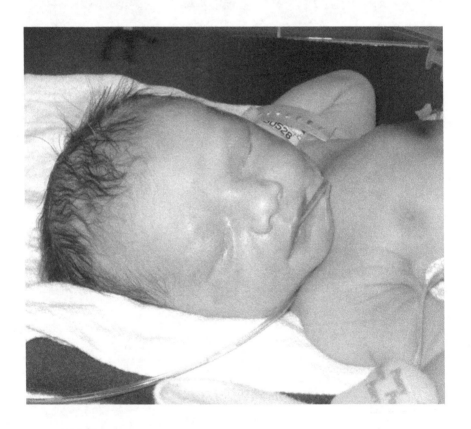